MW01612538

The
THREE *CRUCIAL*
COMMANDS
of CHRIST

with a **Promise**

The
THREE *CRUCIAL*
COMMANDS
of CHRIST
with a **Promise**

Bill C. Dotson

www.hispubg.com

A division of HISpecialists, llc

Copyright © 2014 by Bill C. Dotson

All rights reserved. No portion of this book may be re-produced or utilized in any form or by any means, electronic or mechanical including photocopying, recording or any information storage or retrieval systems without permission in writing from both the copyright owner and the publisher.

Inquiries should be addressed to:
HIS Publishing Group, 1402 Corinth St., Suite 131
Dallas, Texas 75215.

Published by HIS Publishing Group
Division of Human Improvement Specialists, llc
Contact: info@hispubg.com

"Scripture taken from the New King James Version. Copyright © 1982 by Thomas Nelson, Inc. Used by permission. All rights reserved."

Cover Design by Zoe Communications Agency
Cover Image © iStock 2014

ISBN: 978-0-9897398-1-8

Printed and bound in the United States of America

APPRECIATION

My sincere appreciation to three men who assisted
in writing and publishing this book.

Dr. John Tolson, for his encouragement,
contribution to the material and his foreword.

Cecil Price, for his editing.

Larry Luby, for the design and publishing.

DEDICATION

The book is dedicated to my five grandchildren—Luke,
Sarah Peyton, Annie, Will and Renzo.

Go and make disciples!

FOREWORD

You've got to read this book!

I HAVE ALWAYS BEEN INTRIGUED WITH HOW JESUS trained His disciples. In Matthew 28:19 Jesus says, *"Go therefore and make disciples..."* In Matthew 25 Jesus tells the disciples that when He leaves, all hell is going to break loose. So, what did He do in molding them so that when He left and all hell broke loose, they did not fold up and hide?

Now that I have your attention, here's the process:

Matthew 4.17 – Jesus says, *"Repent!"*

Matthew 5-7 – Jesus goes deep inside with the spiritual scalpel and builds the disciples' character.

So when the pressure was on—they showed up and did what Jesus asked them to do— *"Go make disciples!"*

My friend, Bill Dotson, nails it!

You want to help change the planet for Jesus?

Do what Jesus said to do!

You say. "I don't know how." Then learn how!

If we are not making disciples who are making disciples, then we are simply not doing what Jesus told EVERY believer to do!

Thank you, Bill, for this terrific, thoughtful, thorough work!

LET'S GO MAKE DISCIPLES!

Dr. John Tolson
Founder, President
John and Punky Tolson Ministries

CONTENTS

INTRODUCTION

AVE YOU EVER STOPPED AND PONDERED some or all of these thoughts? How can I daily fulfill my destiny? Why did God save me? What is my purpose as a person and as a Christian? Can I really trust my whole life to the Lord? What does that look like? Is He just my Savior and not my Lord and Master? What would give me the greatest satisfaction and sense of accomplishment? What will people, my family, say at my funeral?

Over the many years of reading, studying and meditating on Scripture, I have been most intrigued and motivated by a few verses that seem to me, to sum up the teachings of Jesus that provide the answers to the above questions. Certainly, the Great Commandment in both the Old and New Testaments are central to the life of a Jew or Gentile, but especially to a follower of Christ.

> *"Teacher, which is the great commandment in the law?" 'Jesus said to him, "You shall love the LORD your God with all your heart, with all your soul, and with all your mind. This is*

the first and great commandment. And the second is like it: You shall love your neighbor as yourself. On these two commandments hang all the Law and the Prophets"' (Matthew 22:36–40)

Love is the essential element in all of life. It should be the primary motivation for everything we do and all that we are. But unconditional (agape) love can only emanate from God. So, that is why these two commandments supersede all else. Since we cannot love this way, we obviously must then be a channel for it. But how?

From childhood we also are constantly reminded to live by the Golden Rule:

"Therefore, whatever you want men to do to you, do also to them, for this is the Law and the Prophets" (Matthew 7:12)

Both these and more, many more, direct a way of life and devotion to the Lord. The Ten Commandments were etched in stone for God's chosen people, Israel. The Beatitudes given by Christ in Matthew 5 and Luke 6 are of immense importance to righteousness and holiness for His followers.

The Law given to Moses by God is in and of itself good, but fallen sinners just cannot live up to them.

That is why Jesus had to leave His heavenly residence and step into this world—to fulfill the Law and be the Atonement (God's solution for our sin problem) for us. Sin is a separation from God (spiritual death). Adam's and Eve's disobedience in the Garden of Eden brought about the separation. And we inherited this condition.

> *"For all have sinned and fall short of the glory of God"* (Romans 3:23)

He is loving and holy and made provision for sinful man to have a redeemed relationship with Him.

> *"For the wages of sin is death, but the gift of God is eternal life in Christ Jesus"* (Romans 6:23)

We can't or don't love God with nearly all our being; we don't measure up to the Beatitudes; because of our own selfishness, we don't really honor others more than ourselves and quite honestly, we break the Ten Commandments daily. Some of us don't even love ourselves, so how can I love someone else (neighbor, family) if that poor image exists in my own life. You are probably wondering; so what is the point? Just this: Jesus came to reclaim His Father's creation and to reconcile man to God. And in doing so, He recruited those whom His Father chose for salvation. There was a plan from eternity and you and I were part of it.

Why He would include us, His enemies? I really have no answer, but He did. I plead grace (His unmerited favor) and leave it at that. Every effective commander calls and trains the men suited for the task at hand. There is a defined objective and a mission to be accomplished with a minimum amount of casualties. In the case of the kingdom of God, we really bring no credentials of which to speak, and why Jesus chooses whom He does is nothing short of amazing. God is Sovereign! God's army consists of redeemed people who He calls "His people," even some of which were not originally "His people" (Gentiles who were not of the nation Israel).

He recruited/called (justified) us; He is training (sanctifying) us, and eventually we will be victorious (glorified) in and through Him.

Justification is a legal term whereby we are declared free from all sin and guilt based on the finished work by Jesus on the cross plus zero!

> *"Being justified freely by His grace through the redemption that is in Christ Jesus"* (Romans 3:24)

Sanctification is the process of becoming like Jesus.

"For whom He foreknew, He also predestined to be conformed to the image of His Son..." (Romans 8:29)

Glorification is the end result—becoming like Jesus!

"Being confident of this very thing, that He who has begun a good work in you will complete it until the day of Jesus Christ" (Philippians 1:6)

In the calling and training He set out **three significant** or **crucial commands,** which to me make up our *manual of operations*. As in any branch of military service the serviceman is transformed from a civilian to a "soldier" useful to his superiors and the overall mission, whatever that might be. Obedience is paramount along with the knowledge of their weaponry, commitment to their comrades and oneness toward the common cause. I learned so much about this during basic training. Civilians have more of an independent mindset. We learned that in actual combat this viewpoint leads to defeat. And there is a simple message in the words *basic training*. You start with the basics and build from there.

A short story to better illustrate the point comes from my days as a youth soccer coach with the Dallas Sting. Having coached several teams for quite a few years, it was time to leave it and focus more on work. A new coach was introduced enabling me to move on. About midway into the season, I received a call from a representative of the parents. What I heard concerned me. This really good group of girls was not playing well and losing, to which they were not accustomed. I agreed to return as coach for the remainder of the season. From that first day and for the rest of the practices/games we returned to the basic fundamentals. I emphasized them during every practice. The players responded. We went undefeated the rest of the season. Then, we won the regional championship in Tulsa, and for this age group, it was the Nationals.

Now, fast forward to the mid 2000's. I'm a grandfather watching my oldest grandson get trounced every game for about two years playing soccer. I had long since retired from coaching, but it broke my heart as I saw a talented group of boys who just were not executing basic skills. The following year I was enticed to assist his new head coach who admitted he knew very little about the game. His son was on the team, and he had decided to try to help them. What do you think we started working on right from the start? You guessed it, the basics/fundamentals! They started believing in their abilities and began winning. That year they lost the championship in a shootout. But, the next year, these very same boys won it all. Why? They knew what was expected of them, and they knew how to execute. They had listened well to their coaches and their attention to the basics paid dividends. Now, I have truly permanently retired! That is, unless my other grandchildren need this old man.

As one renowned coach once said: "Football is all about blocking and tackling." Sure, there is an overall game plan, but if players do not understand how to do those basic things, the team's mission will never be accomplished. The same is true in our lives as Christians. We have so much truth in Scripture, all of which is meaningful and pertinent. Sometimes we can get so focused on the forest we lose sight of the trees, which actually comprise the forest. We are involved in great Bible studies and listening to strong preaching on how to live godly lives. All is good, but maybe in the midst of all this, we lose sight of our *basic mission* that Jesus imparted clearly while on Earth.

I have said often that sometimes the most meaningful expressions, and the ones that become imbedded in our minds, are the very first and last ones we receive from someone we have not seen in a while. You naturally hang onto those words that make an impression, whether they were kind or not so kind expressions. Other things that come in between usually fail to have the same impact. They may be meaningful but maybe not as memorable. One of the first things I remember my drill sergeant saying to me was: "Hey boy, get me my clipboard." He was from Oklahoma! I don't think he gave us any parting words, at least none I remember.

And usually if you are just meeting someone for the first time you spend a little time chit–chatting, getting to know the person. When I was young, growing up in Franklin, Tennessee everyone would want to know who your folks were and what high school you attended. Perhaps it has changed over the past sixty years, but that is what I remember then. But that seemed to not be the case with Jesus. He did not major in minor dialogue. Of course, He was/is God so He already knew every single thing about each person He approached or addressed.

So, as He was beginning the last three years of His life, He had little time for idle conversation. He was on a mission, personally, and for His would–be selected followers. There was a purposeful urgency in His life since He knew what He had come to ultimately do. He had an appointed hour of destiny. He had to call His army, train them, sacrifice His life for them and then empower them. If He had had a 3″ x 5″ index card, He might have written these three basic commands on them in order that they, and now we, would never forget. When He approached His first disciples (troops) He did not mince words; nor as He was departing this earth. These are crucial to our life mission as believers.

REPENT — FOLLOW ME — GO!

We will unpack these later but right now I would ask that you pause, speak to Him in prayer and listen to what He is saying to you prior to this short but critical time of "basic training." My prayer for you is that you will never be the "same old civilian" but will join the combat missions of our Lord. And what might that be? An adaptation of John 12:32: *To lift Him up that He may draw men to Himself.* Your complete joy and fulfillment depends on your response to this call, (and maybe even your salvation). If He has enlisted you, then these three commands are your *marching orders. Onward Christian soldier!*

And ladies, where I have used the word, men, it includes you.

CHAPTER ONE
REPENT!

FIRST COMMAND:
"Repent, for the kingdom of God is at hand"
(Matthew 4:17b)

L ET'S LOOK AT HOW *REPENT* IS USED IN THE BIBLE. In the Old Testament the two words where we get our English word *repent* are:

nacham – to be sorry, to console oneself (Strong's 5162)

The Hebrew word naham, is an onomatopoetic term which implies difficulty in breathing, hence, "to pant," "to sigh," "to groan." Naturally it came to signify "to lament" or "to grieve," and when the emotion was produced by the desire of good for others, it merged into compassion and sympathy, and when incited by a consideration of one's own character and deeds it means "to rue," "to repent."[1]

---

[1] [Source: http://topicalbible.org/r/repentance.htm]

shub – to turn back, return (Strong's 7725)

The term *shubh,* is most generally employed to express the Scriptural idea of genuine repentance. It is used extensively by the prophets, and makes prominent the idea of a radical change in one's attitude toward sin and God. It implies a conscious, moral separation, and a personal decision to forsake sin and to enter into fellowship with God. It is employed extensively with reference to man's turning away from sin to righteousness (Deuteronomy 4:30, Nehemiah 1:9; Psalm 7:12; Jeremiah 3:14).[2]

> *Shub* appears more often than *nacham* in the Old Testament.

From the New Testament, the word where we get our English word *repent* is:

> *Metanoeo* – to change one's mind or purpose (Strong's 3340)

The word *metanoeo,* expresses the true New Testament idea of the spiritual change implied in a sinner's return to God. The term signifies "to have another mind," to change the opinion or purpose with regard to

---

[2] Website: http://biblehub.com/topical/r/repentance.htm. Accessed August 20, 2014.

sin. It is equivalent to the Old Testament word "turn." Thus, it is employed by John the Baptist, Jesus, and the apostles (Matthew 3:2; Mark 1:15; Acts 2:38). [3]

In a previous book, *Revival of Repentance,* I defined the word *repent* as used in the New Testament: to "change your mind" and redirect one's life.

The Gospel According to Matthew was written to a Jewish audience. Matthew opened his gospel account with the record of the genealogy demonstrating that Jesus is the promised Jewish Messiah. He held the necessary credentials to sit and rule on David's throne. John the Baptist was the forerunner of Jesus, announcing that their long promised King was now in their midst. The kingdom is *at hand,* or in *their midst,* or *within their grasp,* if they will only receive their Messiah.

And, based on the context, John the Baptist and Jesus are preaching a gospel of repentance directed to the Jewish people and the entire nation, as they needed *to change their minds* about the Messiah, Jesus, as the kingdom of God is within their grasp due to His physical presence with them. Indeed, this is good news.

Again, Jesus is initially offering His kingdom reign only to Israel (see Matthew 10:5, 6). His miracles demonstrated that He was their promised Messiah. Yet, after the nation rejects Christ, following His death on the cross for sin and His resurrection, He commissions the apostles and His followers to preach the gospel

---

[3] Ibid.

message of salvation based on His death and resurrection to both Jews and Gentiles, i.e. all the nations (Matthew 28:19-20).

REPENT... is what John the Baptist preached during his ministry as a precursor to Jesus' ministry. He was a significant prophet; in fact, the last one, excluding our Lord. Why do you think this was the primary, if not sole, message from God through this man crying in the wilderness? Could it have been addressing the chief issue with man, his sinful condition? And could this still be the case for us? Scripture tells us that sin separates us from God. And since He created us, He knows the remedy for our condition. Romans 3:23 reveals that *"for all have sinned and fall short of the glory of God."* We have missed the mark; people who have no "spiritual eyes" to see eternal things such as, for starters, salvation. We don't even know we need a "savior," let alone how to relate to one. We can't recognize that we have been deceived.

Since it is clear that a sinful nature is our primary issue, we need to address the effect and its cure. Repentance has earlier been described as *changing your mind.* Sounds simple enough. But is it really?

Let's trace the term and the process back to its origin in the Bible. In Genesis we are told that God placed the created man, Adam, in the wonderful Garden of Eden, somewhere in Asia. A few specific commands were given to him to maintain a good relationship with his

Creator. Most know the story. Satan tempted Eve; she shared her thoughts and the forbidden fruit with Adam and they both succumbed to the temptation that was placed in front of them. They dropped their eyes off the Lord onto the creation and what it could offer them. Bad idea, for them and all of us! Simply, they disobeyed the few laws God had given them and "sinned"—they became separated from God, and He had to remove them from the Garden. Truly, this was an act of grace by the Lord right from the very start.

The dilemma for a "loving and equally just" God is our predicament. Did the first two humans surprise God? No, but they did disappoint Him. And so do we! For them to be an effective part of His creation, they had to remain obedient. Otherwise, they are a part of the problem, not capable of being useful for kingdom work. Several millennia have passed and it is still the issue—disobedience. It did not take long for sin to corrupt the "first family." Jealousy and anger drove Cain to kill his brother Abel. Satan right now begins "high–fiving" and pumping his fist in the air over this presumed victory. I have heard it said that the devil is smart, but not wise. History has proven that to be true. Oddly, it only says they were ashamed, not repentant.

Fast forward through Genesis to Abraham. Much has transpired since the Garden of Eden dwellers were excommunicated. Noah was asked to obey and build an ark to save his family and the two and four–legged animals from God's plan due to *"the wickedness of man was great on the earth....and that every intent of the thoughts of his heart was only evil continually"'* (Genesis 6:5). This is the strongest evidence of God's view of sin and an unrepentant heart.

"But Noah found grace in the eyes of the LORD... Noah was a just man, perfect in his generations. Noah walked with God" (Genesis 6:8, 9).

Noah was not chosen because he was perfect. He was born of a sinful parentage, as are you and I. Blameless, yes; perfect, no! Blameless in the eyes of God but still a sinful man. Finding favor with God can only be achieved through humility and faith.

"The fear of the Lord is the instruction of wisdom, and before honor is humility" (Proverb 15:33)

I submit that is the case with Noah.

But we were headed toward Abraham (Abram at the time). He was living a "normal pagan life" in Haran with his extended family. One day during his "normal life" God approached him and simply said— "leave the country!" Leave your home and people— lock, stock and barrel! Go *"to a land I will show you"*

(Genesis 12:1). Then He made several promises to Abram at that time—well, actually God pronounced "the blessing for all time." We don't hear of any arguments from him; he just obeyed and left.

Several years go by and God makes a covenant with Abram and the promise of the heir to fulfill the promise. Genesis 15:6 defines faith; ***"And he believed in the LORD, and He accounted it to him as righteousness."*** All this happened in spite of Abraham's and Sarah's laughter (see Genesis 18.10-15) about this most improbable of circumstances. Along the way Sarai's and his name are changed identifying the blessing. One son is born to his wife's handmaiden when the couple tried to help God out with His outlandish promise. I have to ask—do you see yourself in this situation? I see myself. His name was Ishmael. Not the son of the promise although the followers of Islam would argue otherwise.

Then they encounter the "three godly visitors" which deliver the message of the impending pregnancy. A year later Isaac enters the world, just as God ordained and promised. For a few years everything was going along well, until God challenges Abraham's, and I dare say his son's faith, with the command that Abraham sacrifice his beloved son. Again, we see how Abraham responded dutifully to this painful command from his Lord. The son, through whom the promise had been made, was now to be sacrificed. Abraham and Isaac move to the mountainside and prepare the sacrificial altar. Isaac asks where the animal was that they were to be sacrifice. *"...God will provide..."* (Genesis 22:8) is about all his father said. At a time like this few words are expected, as it is too painful for conversation. Can any of you imagine this scene? I can't even let myself go there. Faith in the ultimate sense was at work—in both. But as stated and believed, God did provide a ram caught in a thicket. Test over, settle your hearts, breathe deep and relax. Faith is rewarded! Abraham and Isaac had no way to know about Jesus' future command of "taking up your cross daily" at this time, but believe me, that is what they did that day.

Abraham, the "father of our faith" set the bar or standard very high for us.

"But without faith it is impossible to please Him..." (Hebrews 11:6)

I can quote that verse all day and actually believe it—but when it comes to putting it into action, I fail often and miserably—especially when it is held up against this act of faith. In that test of obedience, Abraham met the test, and so did Isaac. If it all ended there we would have a Hollywood movie of grand proportions. But we later see their humanity surface on several occasions. You would think after surviving this major ordeal victoriously, the rest of the way would be smooth sailing.

Abraham emotionally sacrificed his son to obey God. But we recall earlier, then as Abram, he willingly gave up Sarai to save his skin. The father of our faith wimped out big time in Egypt! I know she was a woman in a male dominated culture and a beautiful one, but she was your wife for heavens' sake. Did he ever repent of this? I see no evidence that he did. I sense even Pharaoh did when he found out she was not his sister. Abram lied, schemed and subjected his wife to possible shame. And we are to embrace him as our role model?

Well, for me it gets even worse. Sometime later in the region of Negev he, now Abraham, did the exact same thing with Abimelech. God spares Abimelech because he acted honorably. And to me, the strangest dialogue happened. Abraham deceived, Sarah went along with it, Abimelech acted righteously and God told him to return her and Abraham would pray for him. Many gifts were bestowed on Abraham and Sarah; and Abraham's prayers for him, his wife and slave girls healed them so they could have more children as God had closed up every womb in Abimelech's household. Abimelech repented and God blessed him and his household. I'm still waiting for Abraham's!

> *"...All things work together for good to those who love God..."* (Romans 8:28a)

Even the schemes of the patriarch were used by God to bring Abimelech to repentance. All I can say is, God is sovereign! (He has supreme power and authority over His creation. (See Isaiah 46:9-10 and Psalm 29:10).

Years later and after the deaths of both Sarah, then Abraham, twins were born to Isaac and Rebekah. They were Esau and Jacob, in that order. We know the story of the deceitful, but successful plan by Jacob and his mother to secure the blessing for him. A major rift ensued. Then we hear that all this had been a part of the "election" by God all along.

> *"Jacob I have loved (chose), but Esau I have hated (rejected)"* (Malachi 1:2b, 3a)

And He told Moses on the mountain; *"I will be gracious to whom I will be gracious, and I will have compassion on whom I will have compassion"* (Exodus 33:19b). Again, God demonstrates His sovereignty. Years pass and the two brothers are about to meet. Jacob encounters God on the way, wrestles all night, and God disjoints his hip. Jacob asks for a blessing and then and there he was told his name was to be changed to Israel. Later at Bethel, according to Genesis 35:10, God officially blessed him as Israel.

Well, the time has now arrived and Jacob is very cautious, as he did not know after all the years apart how his brother would receive him. It tells us that *"He (Jacob) himself went on ahead and bowed down to the ground seven times as he approached his brother"* (Genesis 33:3). Esau was very elated to see him and he ran to meet him, embracing and kissing Jacob. What forgiveness we see here. Jacob was sending much cattle and gifts to Esau who did not want them as he had plenty. But Jacob insisted. His conscience needed cleansing, as I believe he was trying to somehow repay him for stealing the blessing. Jacob insisted and said: *"...If I have now found favor in your sight, then receive my present from my hand, inasmuch as I have seen your face as though I had seen the face of God, and you were pleased with me"* Genesis 33:10). Repentance and forgiveness — what a scene!

Where are we headed with these brief but profound stories? Just this. Repentance, being an act of *changing your mind*, needs to be accompanied with a *change of heart*. *"Faith without works is dead"* (James 2:26b). These acts of repentance could be seen in what they later did. They validated what had gone on in the mind and heart. Repentance is not a mild "I am sorry." God is the judge of our hearts. He needs to see and hear our confessions and cries of repentance and forgiveness, but moreover I submit, it has to be acted out in changed lives.

Dr. Harry Ironside sheds additional light on the subject of repentance: "Literally [repentance] means *a change of mind*. It actually implies a complete reversal of one's inward attitude. To repent is to change one's attitude toward self, toward sin, toward God, toward Christ. . .So to face these tremendous facts is to change one's mind completely, so that the pleasure lover sees and confesses the folly of his empty life; the self-indulgent learns to hate the passions that express the corruption of his nature; the self-righteous sees himself a condemned sinner in the eyes of a holy God; the man who has been hiding from God seeks to find a hiding place in Him; the Christ-rejecter realizes and owns his need of a Redeemer, and so believes unto life and salvation."[4]

Another author adds:

"Repentance is more than a change of mind or feeling sorry for one's sins. It is a radical and deliberate turning or returning to God that results in moral and ethical change and action." [5]

One other patriarch needs to be revisited. God describes David as *"a man after My own heart"* as stated in Acts 13:22. And later we will address Peter. Where

---

[4] Harry A. Ironside, *Except Ye Repent* (Grand Rapids, MI: Baker Book House, 1960), 15,16.

[5] Kenneth Barker, ed. *Zondervan NASB Study Bible* (Grand Rapids: Zondervan, 1999), 1372.

does one start with David? A shepherd, made king of Israel by God, a brilliant commander of Israel's army and a man who wrote numerous Psalms. In my early walk with the Lord, I could not understand this label many teachers and preachers placed on him. You know, he committed two of the "biggies" while king. I couldn't get past this as I was more focused on his actions as opposed to his sorrow. He could have easily justified his actions away as he was king. In a monarchy, we know the king "rules" and answers to no one. But David was no ordinary monarch. His conscience seemed to always be at work. Paul said in Acts 24:16 — *"I myself strive always to have a conscience without offense toward God and men."* I submit the apostle Paul was so aware of the Psalms and the prophetic writings he would have studied David intensely.

God sternly dealt with King David's adultery and murder. The Lord sent Nathan to visit David and truly it was an act of grace in the midst of what David knew about himself, and what he had done. Everything David had committed in secret, God revealed in broad daylight. Nathan pronounces all of the judgment on David and his household and David repents.

> *'Then David said to Nathan, "I have sinned against the LORD..."'* (2 Samuel 12:13)

Notice that no mention was made of the people against whom he had transgressed, even killed, but only that he had sinned against God. This is truth! And he did it instantly. He already knew it in his heart and mind. Don't we? Sure we do. One of the works of the Holy Spirit is to reveal our sins, call them to our conscience, and do what Nathan did. State the obvious; *this is what you have done or not done!*

And then notice the godly sorrow. David wrote Psalm 51 in light of his travail. It is so revealing. This is when I understood why he was "the man after God's own heart." It wasn't his good life in spite of his dastardly deeds; *it was his repentant heart!* Not to justify himself, but to sincerely grieve over his sin against his Lord. There were severe consequences to his sinfulness, but that was not his concern. He had transgressed against God. As stated earlier, sin is separation from God, a falling short of His standards. He is righteous and holy—we are not.

> *"For godly sorrow produces repentance to salvation, not to be regretted; but the sorrow of the world produces death"* (2 Corinthians 7:10)

God–centered sorrow manifests itself by repentance and the experience of divine grace. Notice that the apostle Paul states that godly sorrow produces or brings about repentance, *a change of one's mind* that redirects one's life.

There are many great Psalms penned from the mind and heart of David, but 51 is so transparent as to the meaning of repentance. Let's pull some important phrases from this Psalm. I invite you to read and meditate on its application to you. (Author has taken liberty with the order for emphasis.)

> *Have mercy on me...according to Your*
> *lovingkindness*
> *Blot out my transgressions. . . according to*
> *Your tender mercies*
> *Wash me thoroughly from my iniquity*
> *Cleanse me from my sin*
> *I shall be clean*
> *Wash me and I shall be whiter than snow*
> *Make me to hear joy and gladness*
> *Let the bones You have crushed rejoice*
> *Hide Your face from my sins*
> *Blot out all my iniquities*
> *Create in me a clean heart*
> *Renew a steadfast spirit within me*
> *Do not cast me away from Your presence*
> *Restore to me the joy of Your salvation*
> *Uphold me with Your generous Spirit*
> *Deliver me from bloodguiltiness*
> *Open my lips...*

> *Then I will teach transgressors and sinners*
> *Your ways*
> *Sinners shall be converted to You*
> *My tongue shall sing aloud of Your right*
> *eousness*
> *My mouth shall show forth Your praise*
> *Against You, You only, have I sinned and*
> *done this evil in Your sight.*

The understanding that David reveals is straight from the throne room of God.

> *"For You do not desire sacrifice, or else I would give it; You do not delight in burnt offering. The sacrifices of God are a broken spirit; a broken and a contrite heart— These, O God, You will not despise"* (Psalm 51:16, 17)

We talked briefly about the need to see evidence of a changed heart and mind. David declares that he will spend his remaining time teaching others and singing His praises. A forgiven king just became a disciple maker and praise leader!

Oswald Chambers states in *My Utmost for His Highest* on November 28 the following. "The greatest blessing spiritually is the knowledge that we are *destitute;* until we get there our Lord is powerless." He is so correct and David exemplifies this in his repentant prayer.

Before we get to Peter, maybe we should make a brief stop in history and examine Isaiah. From chapters 1 through 5 we read of the condition of Israel's heart and the consequences of their sinful life. At the beginning of chapter 6, God visits His temple where Isaiah was probably praying. He says that he saw God in all His holiness. Knowing he fit right in with his people and their transgressions, Isaiah instantly knew the consequences of seeing God as a sinful man. He feared instant death, if not severe punishment.

> *"Woe to me! For I am undone! Because I am a man of unclean lips...my eyes have seen the King, the LORD of hosts"* (v. 5)

<u>Repentance!</u> As he was surely waiting for the sentence to be announced and executed, a completely different thing happens.

> *'Then one of the seraphim flew to me having in his hand a live coal in his hand, which he had taken with tongs from the altar. And he touched my mouth with it and said, "Behold, this has touched your lips; your iniquity is taken away and your sin purged"'* (vv. 6, 7)

<u>Forgiveness</u>! Unmerited <u>grace!</u>

Now we get to witness a repentant and forgiven heart respond to this unmerited forgiveness. God speaks and asks, *"Whom shall we send? And who will go for us?"* Guess who volunteers willingly? Right, Isaiah! He replies: *"Here am I. Send me"* (v. 8). This is another evidence of deeds reflecting repentance through faith. David and Isaiah were operating out of grace for the remainder of their lives. Not perfectly, just willingly!

We could easily examine Job, Jonah, King Saul, and even Judas Iscariot. Each repented but with dissimilar endings to their lives. Remember, there are still consequences to our sins.

Several decades later the last prophet came preaching repentance. John, the baptizer, was preparing the way for the "new covenant." In a sense, he was also the "announcer" of what was to come. Like in any stage show, the minor acts come first, setting the stage for the main act. In this case, that would be Jesus. As with John, Jesus continued this essential element of salvation and all it entails. One of the disciples that Jesus called was Simon, later to be identified as Peter. A fisherman and I dare say a successful one. He had been called out from his business and told to repent because the kingdom of heaven was near. Not only was it near, He (the Word) was speaking to him. They spend three interesting years together with Jesus discipling him and the others. Peter had seen how Jesus dealt with sinful people, was in the inner circle of three (Peter,

James and John), and showed a lot of leadership. Of course, as with many of us "Type A" personalities, our foot gets caught in our mouths way too often. Peter was no different.

Using some sanctified imagination, Peter probably thought: "Jesus, anywhere you go, I go. Anything you do, count me in. I have your back; with You all the way. I am Yours and You are mine; and I will never deny knowing You, no matter the cost. Count on me when the going gets tough." Unfortunately, when it did, the "tough one" wimped out! Not once, not twice, but three times he denied even knowing Jesus. Sadness enters into his life once he heard the cock crow. Time to confess and repent, Peter! Can you even imagine how sorrowful he must have been? It was not like he could approach Jesus the next morning. He was tried, crucified, dead and buried. Peter is so distraught over his sinful actions. Miserable comes to mind. All night long and for the next several days he had to deal with his denials. This "powerful" disciple was brought low and he needed some old–fashioned comforting.

Christ is resurrected and re-encounters the disciples, including Peter in John 21. Jesus asked Peter: *"Do you love Me, Peter?"* Jesus asked three times. Is it coincidental that it matched the number of times he denied Him? I think not. But it also points out that Jesus wanted Peter to experience the depth of his call to discipleship. Every time he was asked, it had to drive the nail deeper into his heart. And each time Jesus gave him the mandate for him to carry out for the rest of his life. The Lord's mandate was: **Feed My lambs, tend My sheep, and feed My sheep.** Peter was now broken; contrition had settled in and Jesus knew He had a faithful apostle in the making. Peter's lifelong mission (his deeds) reflected a man who had encountered the depth of repentance—and he had received comfort/peace through forgiveness.

We could go on with these stories of brokenness that produced usable disciples for the Lord. But I think you get the picture. The need for repentance entered the scene very early on with Adam and Eve, our original parents. Nothing has changed nor will it until the Lord returns. It is simply God's mechanism for fallen man to be reconciled to Him, <u>daily</u>. Repentance would not be available to us had it not been for the Atonement (Christ's death on the cross). God can receive our petitions for forgiveness because of His Son's, our Savior's sacrificial death. Jesus knew what He had come to earth to eventually do. So, it was important that His soon–to–be apostles would have a clear understanding of what comes first in the relationship with His Father. His very first command was—"REPENT!" And we will see that it is not just a once in a lifetime action—it is daily, if not more often.

I was once taught through the means of two circles being drawn.

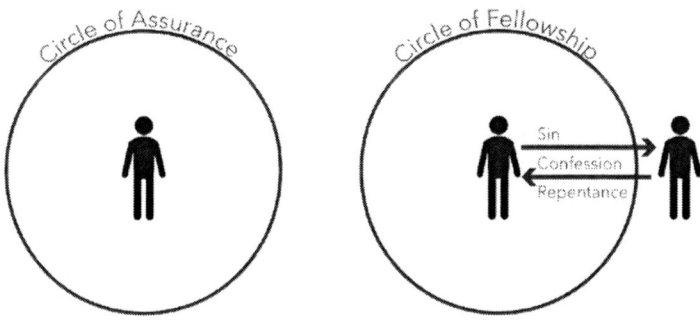

THE CIRCLES OF ASSURANCE AND FELLOWSHIP

The first was the circle of assurance; the other, the circle of fellowship. Once we have trusted Christ for our salvation through the process of justification, we are secure in that salvation evidenced by several of Jesus' teachings. Simply, we cannot fall out of the circle of assurance. But, we can fall out of the circle of fellowship with Him, actually His Spirit. We cannot fall from grace, but we can fall with grace. Our disobedience, rebellion and transgressions grieve the Spirit.

> *"The spirit indeed is willing, but the flesh is weak."* (Matthew 26:41b)

Confession is the first step of moving back into our "circle." Confess means *agree with*. He has made provision for us.

"If we confess our sins, He is faithful and just to forgive our sins and to cleanse us from all unrighteousness" (1John 1:9)

God already knows; we are simply agreeing with what He knows. One of the works of the Spirit is to bring to our conscious minds the sins in our lives; not to slam us, but to redeem/restore the relationship. It is His way of keeping our relationship on track. Trains run off the tracks and so do we. Train wrecks are usually not a pretty sight—and so are similar mishaps in our own lives.

Oh, it is well to revisit Peter two months later. Jesus had since ascended back to His Father. Pentecost had occurred with the Holy Spirit being poured out on the disciples as prophesied. Peter and the others were now assimilating all they had been taught by Jesus. Peter had sinned greatly, had repented and been forgiven by the Lord—now being filled with the Holy Spirit, he was about the work left for him to do; feeding Christ's sheep. And what sermon does he start preaching? The gospel message—*Christ died for our sins and rose from the dead.* [6] We see this recorded early in the Book of Acts. In chapter two he addresses the crowd and presents a challenge to them.

---

[6] Summary of the gospel message by R. Larry Moyer, founder of Evantell, Inc., Dallas, Texas.

"Therefore let all the house of Israel know assuredly that God has made this Jesus, whom you crucified, both Lord and Christ." 'Now when they heard this, they were cut to the heart, and said to Peter and the rest of the apostles, "Men and brethren, what shall we do?"' 'Peter said to them, "Repent and let every one of you be baptized, in the name of Jesus Christ for the remission of your sins; and you shall receive the gift of the Holy Spirit. For the promise is for you and to your children, and all who are afar off, as the Lord will call"' (vv. 2:36–39)

Do we see how this applies to us? When we are faced with the awareness of our sins; what shall we do? John the Baptist, then Jesus, then a Spirit-filled Peter says: **REPENT!**

While we briefly described repentance at the beginning of the chapter, I think it is well to examine it in more detail, as it is so important to salvation and discipleship, and all that entails. It is God's provision for a Spirit–filled, victorious life honoring to God and impacting our world! While we could look at Webster's Dictionary, Scripture oftentimes reveals "godly sorrow" in repentance, but as I stated in *Revival of Repentance* a "change of mind" that redirects one's life is the best definition. Some of the people have already been discussed who suffered for their sinfulness and experienced this sorrow. To be sure, we may be "grieving painfully for sin against a holy God." It is godly sorrow that should lead to repentance; to change one's mind and redirect one's life **in response to God's revealed truth in the Bible.** It is certainly not "sugar-coating" our transgressions. This could never lead us to the place where we need to go. A band–aid works on a scratch; but cancer usually requires surgery! Unfortunately, most of the time we as self–centered humans justify away our failures to live holy lives. With our eyes on the world and others, we simply cannot even recognize sin in our life. "I'm not as bad as some and certainly no worse than most."

But when we redirect our eyes to the Word, and the Holy Spirit starts convicting us of our shortcomings, it is then we start "seeing" our true state.

> *"Looking unto Jesus, the author and finisher (pioneer and perfecter) of our faith..."* (Hebrews 12:2a)

While the Spirit does convict us, He is also our Helper, our Comforter. If I am experiencing godly sorrow with the need to repent, then my need is to be undergirded by a "Godly Comforter." But repentance is an act of the will. I really need to want to be cleansed and sense an abiding relationship with Him and others. The following are some verses that reveal this sorrow.

> *"For I am ready to fall, and my sorrow is continually before me"* (Psalm 38:17)

> *"I would comfort myself in sorrow; my heart is faint in me"* (Jeremiah 8:18)

> *"When he heard this, he became very sorrowful for he was very rich"* (Luke 18:23)

> *"That I have great sorrow and continual grief in my heart"* (Romans 9:2)

> *"For I have satiated the weary soul, and I have replenished every sorrowful soul"* (Jeremiah 31:25)

> *"The sorrows of Sheol surrounded me; the snares of death confronted me"* (2 Samuel 22:6)

There is no better example of repentance than in 2 Corinthians 7. We will examine this with the hope that we can come away with a clear picture and how we should respond to our sinfulness and a holy God.

"Therefore, having these promises, beloved, let us cleanse ourselves from all filthiness of the flesh and spirit, perfecting holiness in the fear of God" (v. 1)

What promises? Maybe it will help us to look back at them. In the previous chapter starting in v. 16 Paul addresses them this way, *"And what agreement has the temple of God with idols? For you are the temple of the living God..."* (author emphasis). This is such a deep theological statement of truth it bears some thought. If we are, and we are, the "temple" where God resides; then it would stand to reason that as "priests" of God, we need to be holy vessels. So, when "sin" of any nature is revealed within us by His Spirit, we need to proceed with a "ceremony" of cleansing. God's gift of grace to us is—*confession and repentance*. This was only made possible by Jesus through the Atonement, but it accrues to us as His people.

Paul goes on and shares what the Lord has said in times past.

"I will dwell with them and walk among them. I will be their God and they shall be My people" (v. 16b)

Yahweh stated earlier:

"Come out from among them and be separate says the Lord. Do not touch what is unclean, and I will receive you. I will be a Father to you, and you shall be My sons and daughters says the LORD Almighty" (2 Corinthians 6:17, 18)

Can you see the picture? Above, we are shown to be His temple, and now He shares that we are to separate from the evil and He will walk among us, even as a Father, as sons and daughters. Holy means "set apart." This is what He is calling us to; *"be in the world but not of the world"* (author's paraphrase of John 17:16). And the provision He has made for us when we fail and fall short to be restored is — *repentance.*

Back now to 2 Corinthians 7; Paul addresses the central issue, that of godly sorrow being the catalyst of repentance. Look with me in verses 9 and 10. *"Now I rejoice, not that you were made sorry,* **but that your sorrow led to repentance.** *For you were made sorry in a godly manner, that you might suffer loss in us for nothing. For godly sorrow produces repentance leading to salvation, not to be regretted; but the sorrow of the world produces death."*

My translation is: **revealed sin leads to godly sorrow--that leads to repentance--that leads to life!** Our hope is in the Atonement and resurrection, not in wishful thinking! That is why we can *"...come boldly to the throne of grace..."* (Hebrews 4:16).

If we take this a little further, maybe we can get the clearest picture of all. A pattern of life is shown here. I'm sad because I got caught with my hand in the cookie jar. I'm frightened because I got caught cheating on a pop quiz. I'm really despondent after being arrested for a DWI. I'm feeling so dirty after being caught cheating on my wife. I am near suicide having been caught stealing from the company over the past ten years. I sense hopelessness from becoming addicted to alcohol and drugs and losing my family. All of these may or may not lead to godly sorrow. But I would suggest the earlier in life we learn to truly repent the better.

But what if you had never done any of these and you were falsely accused of doing all of them and much more? And to add insult to injury, you are asked to pay for these crimes and transgressions you absolutely did not commit, either with prison time and/or financial repayment. And because the judge and jury wanted to make a statement, they give you life with no parole. I just read recently of two Texas inmates who were cleared by DNA from their trial 30 years ago. What mixed emotions they must feel. But consider how they must have felt serving this time knowing they were completely innocent. Anger would be a mild expression!

Well, this happened two thousand years ago, at a time when capital punishment was much more prevalent than in America today. The Roman government used crucifixion to get rid of these criminals. It made a strong statement to the general public. Jesus was living at this time and was accused of multiple crimes, none of which were true. Not by the Romans, but by His own people, the Jews. Again, the nation Israel rejected Jesus Christ, their promised Messiah. Enter—godly sorrow—with a capital "G!" The Son of God was to be executed for the sins of the world, yours and mine, not one of which was His own as He lived a perfectly sinless life. Earlier that week He had actually wept over Jerusalem, displaying Godly sorrow over their blindness to truth. The same people He was weeping for were now calling for His death.

We see that Christ was not sorrowful for Himself or for His mistakes as a man, but for those He came to save. And He never wavered in obedience. He loved His Father with an everlasting love. He did not want to disappoint or disobey Him. How many of you have experienced this deep love and loyalty to your mom or dad or someone dear to you? When Jesus struggled in the Garden of Gethsemane and sweated blood over the upcoming torture as a man, He at the same time was experiencing Godly sorrow for you and me. His obedience and eventual death did not require repentance. He had done nothing for which to repent.

But what He did do was to make salvation available to us. He was in the world reconciling us to His Father. *Repentance is a part of reconciliation.* The shed blood of our Lord and Savior made provision for this to happen. How else can fallen sinners ever function without it? Hunters and soldiers know one must always be careful to maintain their weapon; that is, cleaning it. To be useful and effective it has to be able to function properly. So with us! Unconfessed sin in our lives is like a dirty barrel and a clogged cylinder. We need to praise God that He uses His Spirit to bring to our mind the sins of omission and co-mission. David knew this.

"Who can understand his errors? Cleanse me from secret faults. Keep back Your servant from presumptuous sins; let them not have dominion over me" (Psalm 19:12, 13a)

Grace is seen in the act of repentance. We don't deserve the provisions of repentance, but Jesus made it possible. "Undeserved merit" is an oft–used definition. Can you even imagine 70–80 years of living in darkness and bondage as a believer? Unable to be usable for your Lord and Master would be a life full of disappointment and heartbreak. He knows this dilemma and His love afforded a remedy. A bathtub that has been used to wash a dirty person has a plug and a drain. Who would not want to immediately remove the filthy water for the next bath, for your use or the use of others? The longer the dirty water remains in the tub, the harder it is to clean it. A soap ring develops and after a while hardens. It then requires a lot of elbow grease after the water is able to drain. It's the same with us! This image should lead us to keep short accounts of our grievances and sins. To deal with them as soon as we become aware through the Spirit's leading is a recipe for successful cleansing. Based on this example— repentance is likened unto a "spiritual drain" with a "built-in cleansing agent!" DRANO!!! That is "tub" lingo for Hallelujah!

As stated earlier, the first step in the act of repentance is *confession*. Much can be said about this but it is simply "agreeing with God." Nothing is hidden from Him—so, confessing is stating what He already knew; and you now know needs addressing. We commit individual sins; we need to confess them in the same manner.

Even though Jesus' original words were for the Jewish nation, we can draw a Biblical principle that He desires all people to repent, to change our minds about Him, and trust or receive Him as their personal Savior.

Sadly, some Bible teachers, preachers, and authors believe one must *repent* (with the meaning of cleaning up one's life) before a person can believe or receive the gospel. This prerequisite is a human work than adds to the gospel of grace. A Nashville friend of mine would say: "God don't clean His fish before He catches them."

Dr. Larry Moyer, the CEO of Evantell, Inc., in Dallas provides Biblical insight on repentance in their evangelism seminar workbook: "Repentance, when used in an evangelistic context in Scripture means 'to change your mind about whatever is keeping you from trusting Christ and trust Him to save you.'" Dr. Moyer elaborates: "When an individual has changed his mind about whatever is keeping him from trusting Christ and trusts Him to save him, both repentance and faith have taken place."[7]

To close this chapter, I refer to a summation statement that seems to completely describe the act of repentance.

> "Repentance is a heartfelt sorrow for sin, a renouncing of it, and a sincere commitment to forsake it and walk in obedience to Christ." [8]

Before we move to the next crucial command of Christ, I think it would be wise to examine our own hearts. It is fine to look at all the people we have discussed and just studied but what it all boils down to is—how does this apply to me?

---

[7] R. Larry Moyer and Cam Abell. *You Can Tell It! Mini-Seminar in Personal Evangelism* (Dallas, TX: Evantell, Inc., 2006), 10.

[8] Wayne Grudem, *Systematic Theology: An Introduction to Biblical Doctrine* (Grand Rapids, MI: Zondervan, 2006), 713.

QUESTIONS TO CONSIDER:

What do you consider the areas of repentance you need to address?

Does pride stand in your way of confession?

What experiences have you had in the past where the need to repent surfaced?

Did your relationship with God and others change?

If so, in what way?

What did the Spirit teach you in this chapter?

How will it affect you going forward?

How sorry should I be for my sins and for how long?

CHAPTER TWO
FOLLOW ME!

SECOND COMMAND:

"...Follow Me, and I will make you fishers of men"
(Matthew 4:19)

*F*OLLOW ME...IS AN INVITATION AND ALSO A command. Hostesses at any restaurant lead the way to a table and you follow. Not that you couldn't do it by yourself but she knows the table that she wants you to use. In a funeral procession we follow the hearse; in the armed services, we follow those in leadership over us; as you sing in a choir you follow the director; and in a marching band the drum major is directing you. All through life most of us are following something or somebody much of the time, even when you are the leader. To be a follower is a normal role in life. For the most part, we are easily led; like into a poor investment, a false sense of security; like sheep to a slaughter. Ask the German people about following their misguided and deranged 20th century fuehrer, Adolf Hitler.

"My sheep hear My voice, and I know them, and they follow Me" (John 10:27)

In the Bible, Jesus spoke about a true shepherd and a false one. The sheep know the voice of their shepherd as he has only their best interests so they follow him. But the hired sheepherder does not have the same interest; when the wolf comes around he abandons them and leaves them for the wolf to devour. So, as we move through life we have to become attuned to the voice of the One who we are following. It is called trust.

Also, there is a need to understand the purpose of the mission. I'm going to the table—to dine. I'm following the drum major to execute a coordinated routine and play beautiful music. Why is Jesus asking you and me to follow Him? He does not leave it to guesswork. He spells it out—to make us *fishers of men.* But what does it mean and what price are we being asked to pay? A precision halftime marching band presentation doesn't just happen. Just before the 2011 Cotton Bowl three of our grandchildren, accompanied by their mother, went to see the widely heralded Fightin' Texas A & M Aggie Band practice at a high school field. They came away with a new appreciation for the work that goes into their performances. And it even goes far deeper than even what they observed. The early mornings and late nights, the hours of studying the precision movements, not counting the hours practicing their music.

One director of the band with a vision for the end result leads each band member and together they follow him to accomplish the mission. The snare drummer cannot go off on his own or the trumpet player his during the performance. They each have been trained to hear his voice and collectively follow his lead. The body of Christ is no different. Each of us is gifted differently as He directs us through His Spirit to follow Him and play as one.

So, before we go farther maybe we should know more. Who is the One asking me to follow Him; what are the costs involved and what is to be the outcome? And whom is He following? Let's deal with these separately. Oswald Chambers has some interesting thoughts on this matter.

THE LIFE OF POWER TO FOLLOW
January 5

Jesus answered him, 'Where I am going you cannot follow Me now, but you shall follow Me afterward' (John 13:36)

"And when He had spoken this, He said to him, 'Follow Me' " (John 21:19). Three years earlier Jesus had said, "Follow Me" (Matthew 4:19), and Peter (John 21:19) followed with no hesitation. The irresistible attraction of Jesus was upon him and he did not need the Holy Spirit to help him do it. Later he came to the place where he denied Jesus, and his heart broke. Then he received the Holy Spirit and Jesus said again, "Follow Me" (John 21:19). Now no one is in front of Peter except the Lord Jesus Christ. The first "Follow Me" was nothing mysterious; it was an external following. Jesus is now asking for an internal sacrifice and yielding (see John 21:18).

Between these two times Peter denied Jesus with oaths and curses (see Matthew 26:69-75). But then he came completely to the end of himself and all of his self-sufficiency. There was no part of himself he would ever rely on again. In his state of destitution, he was finally ready to receive all that the risen Lord had for him. "…He breathed on them, and said to them, 'Receive the Holy Spirit'" (John 20:22). No matter what changes God has performed in you, never rely on them. Build only on a Person, the Lord Jesus Christ, and on the Spirit He gives.

All our promises and resolutions end in denial because we have no power to accomplish them. When we come to the end of ourselves, not just mentally but completely, we are able to "receive the Holy Spirit." *"Receive the Holy*

Spirit"—the idea is that of invasion. There is now only One who directs the course of your life, the Lord Jesus Christ. [9]

Yes, Mr. Chambers, the who is Jesus Christ, the only Son of God—fully God and perfect man! He has the authority given to Him by the Father.

"And they were astonished at His teaching, for His word was with authority" (Luke 4.32)

And even stronger evidence is presented.

"For as the Father has life in Himself, so He has granted the Son to have life in Himself, and has given Him authority to execute judgment also, because He is the Son of Man" (John 5.26, 27)

We will see this in more detail in the third chapter but Jesus spoke of His authority as He was leaving earth.

'And Jesus came and spoke to them, saying, "all authority has been given to Me in heaven and on earth"' (Matthew 28:18)

---

[9] Oswald Chambers, *My Utmost For His Highest*, January 5.

At the very end of chapter 12 of John, Jesus makes it abundantly clear as to where He is getting His authority to teach.

> *"For I have not spoken on My own authority; but the Father who sent Me gave Me a command, what I should say and what I should speak. And I know that His command is everlasting life. Therefore, whatever I speak, just as the Father has told Me, so I speak"* (vv. 49, 50)

Also, in Luke 4:17–21, He reads from the scroll of *"fulfilled in your hearing."* What they heard was the prophecy of the coming Messiah.

Can there be any doubt that Jesus was the long–awaited Messiah, the Christ? The scriptural evidence presented here is only the small tip of the iceberg. Simply, the Bible is all about His Father and Him and their plan of creation and redemption. But He does go on to express what I believe is such an affirmation by Him of who He was/is.

"I and My Father are one" (John 10:30)

He was defending His claim to be the Christ by asking them to believe His works, if not His words. As do so many people in the world today and throughout history, the crowd present picked up stones to stone

Him. Which gives us the opportunity to examine the costs associated with following Jesus today.

> *"And he who does not take his cross and follow after Me is not worthy of Me"* (Matthew 10:38)

Doesn't sound like an invitation to a beach vacation! We see earlier that His enemies were ready to stone Him for speaking truth about Himself. And these same men eventually were the ones who crucified Him. Don't get too settled in and comfortable because you are removed from the scene by over 2,000 years. Jesus tells us in Matthew 5:11 something we need to hear and at the same time might be concerned about.

> *"Blessed are you when they revile and persecute you, and say all kinds of evil against you falsely for My sake."*

When is the last time you felt blessed as someone was reaming you out for your faith? Seems like an oxymoron on the surface. Jesus told the disciples:

> *"Remember the word that I said to you, 'A servant is not greater than his master.' If they persecuted Me, they will also persecute you'"* (John 15:20a)

Ready to enlist yet?

Before you decide, please know that you did not choose Him, He chose you! Did you know that, or if you did, do you believe it? So many Christians have the false impression that "they made a decision for Christ." You may have trusted Him after the Holy Spirit enlightened you as to the gospel, but you and I did not do the choosing. Why? *"Lest no man should boast."* (Take a look at Ephesians 2:8, 9). How can a "man dead in his trespasses" make any "decision?" He can't and doesn't. Why stress this theological issue, Bill? Because it bears greatly on the calling the Lord places on your life. He does the calling and ensures you are equipped for the journey. Listen to what Jesus said in John 15:16.

"You did not choose Me, but I chose you and appointed you that you should go and bear fruit, and that your fruit should remain, that whatever you ask the Father in My name He may give you."

Any further questions?

Did Andrew or Peter or Matthew or John, and later Paul—did any of the disciples call Jesus to come into their life and change them forever? Jesus saw each and said simply, but profoundly, "Follow Me!" No arguments or hesitations are recorded in Scripture. I invite you to prayerfully read Luke 5:1–11. Three fishermen

(Peter, James, and John) left their nets after they heard Jesus say: *"Do not be afraid, from now on you will catch men"* (v. 10b). Faith replaced fear. What were they thinking? What did they see? Remember Abram (Abraham) putting up any argument when God called him to leave everything dear to him and go to live in tents for the remainder of his life? He is the "father of our faith." Jesus secured our faith with His life, death and resurrection. So, were they convinced of this fact when they "dropped their nets" and followed Him? I doubt it. What are your thoughts right now? Has this challenge been issued to you; and if so, what is your response? Be honest!

If you are wavering, hang on, as it may get a bit more challenging. No bed to lie on, no real home; deny yourself! What a way to recruit enlistees. No medical program, no earthly retirement plan, vacation time can wait, no sick leave, give away all you have, love your enemies who are trying to do you in, forgive 490 times, walk two miles if only asked to go one, give the shirt off your back—no, even your new leather jacket, feed the poor, lose your life to gain it, hate your parents; well at least don't love them more than Jesus! Shall I go on? Now, do you see why He has to do the choosing and calling? No one in their right mind would volunteer for this life assignment on their own; unless, unless they sensed something, someone, some cause greater than themselves. That has to be what the first disciples saw in Him; it just has to be. And honestly, living under the oppressive rule of the Romans and their taxation was a formula for something different.

I am sure Jesus did not tell them everything at once. He even allowed them to believe that an earthly kingdom might be in store and an overthrow of the Romans. One even wanted a piece of the action financially—while two wanted seats of authority right next to Jesus. Is that what we want from our Lord? Blessings upon blessings! Not You, Jesus, just the blessings. But lest we misread His call, He said—"Follow *Me*." To do what? No, that is a wrong question. To make me what? To make us "fishers of men" is His objective. And He declares that He <u>will</u> do the making. He calls, and He makes! But as we see above; we may not have anything of the world and we are going to be persecuted along the way. So, what is His plan and provisions for this rag–tag army? Answer: HIMSELF!

To fathom this we might examine what He said about HIMSELF:

> I am the bread of life
> I am living water
> I am the Light of the world
> I am the way
> I am the truth
> I am the life
> I am the resurrection

I am the door
I am the veil
I am the Good Shepherd

And even more emphatic were the words God spoke from heaven about Him as He was ascending from His baptism by John.

"...You are My beloved Son, in whom I am well pleased" (Mark 1:11)

On the Mount of Transfiguration, the three disciples saw and heard the same words spoken by God the Father about Jesus and telling them to "listen to Him." It would seem to me that if His Father was well pleased with Him, why would we not trust Him with our very lives when He invites us to follow Him.

And not only do we see who He was/is, we are made abundantly aware of what He was about during His earthly ministry, and now through us in the power and presence of His Holy Spirit. Scripture records the following. But He also told the disciples that He had to go away, back to His Father, in order that greater works could be done—in and through us. In plain and simple language: "You ain't seen nothing yet!" At the end of The Gospel According to John we hear that the things recorded about Him are mere sketches of the magnitude of His works while on earth.

*"And there are also many other things that Je-
sus did, which if they were written one by
one, I suppose that even the world itself could
not contain the books that would be written.
Amen"* (John 21:25)

And Amen! And He tells us that even greater things
will be done through His Spirit, and evidently in and
through us. Is that why He possibly asked us to follow
Him? So that our lives would take on the miraculous
and the fullness only He can offer. Paul said it well in
Romans 8, *"For I consider that the sufferings of this
present time are not worthy to be compared with the
glory which shall be revealed in us."*

*"Go your way; behold, I send you out as
lambs among wolves"* (Luke 10:3)

Pastors in Sudan actually carry their burial shroud
with them in the predominately Muslim areas. They
realize that death is a strong possibility and all they ask
is their assassins give them a decent burial. Is that what
it means to "follow Me?" How many of us have signed
on for this level of commitment? Jesus surely tells us,
*"...If anyone desires to come after Me, let him deny
himself, and take up his cross, and follow Me. For
whoever desires to save his life will lose it, but whoever loses his life for My sake will find it"* (Matthew

16:24, 25). What do you think; did the pastors get it? The more important question is: Do we? Most of the world's Christians are not asked to "carry their burial shroud" but it is the attitude, the mindset that Jesus is after. What are we clutching that needs to be released? Each one of us has our idols that we cling to for security, even for life itself. Am I really "crucified with Christ" to the point I no longer have any hang–ups with following Him "daily" as He addresses in Luke 9:23? He may not call all of us to some desolate spot of the world, but He does give us the clear command for all of us in Romans 12:1, 2:

> *"I beseech you therefore, brethren, by the mercies of God, that you present your bodies a living sacrifice, holy, acceptable to God, which is your reasonable service. And do not be conformed to this world, but be transformed by the renewing of your mind, that you may prove what is that good and acceptable and perfect will of God."*

Before we volunteer for this lifetime excursion, we need to consider one more of His admonitions.

> *"So likewise, whoever of you does not forsake all that he has cannot be My disciple"* (Luke 14:33)

Luke had earlier recorded Jesus' words being a little more specific and personal as it relates to *all*. Beginning in Luke 14:26, 27 we see that He addressed great multitudes with a very powerful gut–wrenching statement.

"If anyone comes to Me and does not hate his father and mother, wife and children, brothers and sisters, yes, and his own life also, he cannot be My disciple. And whoever does not bear the cross and come after Me cannot be My disciple."

He is painting a clear picture and presenting the ultimate challenge in order for us to make the decision to follow Him. The Marines want "a few good men." And so does Jesus!

There is a well–documented story of the first year the legendary Paul "Bear" Bryant took over the Texas Aggies as head football coach in 1954. Over 100 football players went to the training camp in Junction, Texas but as it turned out, it was no ordinary camp. He was establishing a program to become a winner. He had to know who was up to the task, who was 'all in'. It must have been weeks of near hell for the group of young aspiring football players. They were tested in every way. Some reported issues were—114° summer heat and deprived of food and water for hours of grueling practice each day. Only 35 survived and they became known as the "The Junction Boys." A movie of the same name was later produced in 2002. The "multitude" had dwindled to a few. If you are interested, they won only one game that year but the survivors became the nucleus of the team who two years later went undefeated and became champions.

Do you see the corollary between these "boys" and Jesus' disciples? Our Lord wanted to see who would return with Him to take up their cross. As with The Junction Boys who became the nucleus of the Fightin' Aggies, so did the disciples who chose to follow Him. They may not have been very impressive to start with, but today the church is still in the game and make up the Lord's "winning team." Unlike Coach Bryant who left A & M after three years, Jesus is still our "Head Coach" after 2,000 years plus, fulfilling His promise to "never leave us or forsake us." He has even sent a "Strong Assistant" to ensure we can follow Him and even succeed. The Holy Spirit is that assistant. But He is much more than that; He is truly God and He knows the game plan and our assignments well!

The early disciples would not have been able to fulfill the call to follow Jesus without the power from the Spirit. Only after Pentecost did these ordinary men become the "nucleus." A few good men had now become empowered. Timidity turned to boldness. Truth they had learned earlier now became life changing, for them and those they encountered. Following Him took on a whole new look, and their mission for life. It can for us too. But what were these disciples looking for that drove most of them to experience martyrdom? Just this: heavenly treasure as opposed to earthly. Jesus said,

"In My Father's house are many mansions; if it were not so, I would have told you. I go to prepare a place for you. And if I go and prepare a place for you, I will come again and receive you to Myself; that where I am, there you may be also. And where I go you know, and the way you know" (John 14:2–4)

Exchange your earthly fishing boat for a mansion in heaven was their choice. But what they and we are getting is—Jesus—for eternity. Temporal versus eternal! No contest they said! Bring it on! *Ordinary fishermen were transformed into extraordinary fishers of men!*

And to conclude we go back to the father of our faith, Abraham. The writer of Hebrews under the direction of the Spirit shows us the mindset of faith.

"By faith he dwelt in the land of promise as in a foreign country, dwelling in tents with Isaac and Jacob, the heirs with him of the same promise; for he waited for the city which has

foundations, whose builder and maker is God" (vv. 11:9, 10)

Why would he leave Haran, his family and possessions except there was a better reward? Only eyes of faith would see that. And not only Abraham, but also all who have followed since him, some of which are listed in the "gallery of faith" a few verses later in Hebrews.

"These all died in faith, not having received the promises, but having seen them afar off were assured of them, embraced them and confessed that they were strangers and pilgrims on the earth. For those who say such things declare plainly that they seek a homeland. And truly if they had called to mind that country from which they had come out, they would have had opportunity to return. But now they desire a better, that is, a heavenly country. Therefore God is not ashamed to be called their God, for He has prepared a city for them" (Hebrews 11:13–16)

It is called "deferred gratification!"

To follow Jesus in our flesh is impossible. Peter tried it, and it didn't work as we saw earlier. But Jesus told His followers who were addressing Him along with the rich young ruler that *"...With men it is impossible, but not with God, for with God all things are possible"* (Mark 10:27). Interestingly, Jesus was saying to the young ruler to sell all he had, give it to the poor, in exchange for treasure in heaven, and come take up your cross and "follow Me."

> *"But he was sad at this word, and went away sorrowful. . ."* (Mark 10:22)

Will we? I trust not.

And let us conclude this chapter with the following challenge. These verses address the true cost of discipleship. Will you see yourself in any of these?

> *"Now it happened as they journeyed on the road, that someone said to Him, "Lord, I will follow You wherever You go." And Jesus said to him, "Foxes have holes and birds of the air have nests, but the Son of Man has nowhere to lay His head." Then He said to another, "Follow Me." But he said, "Lord, let me first go and bury my father." Jesus said to him, "Let the dead bury their own dead, but you go and preach the kingdom of God." And another also said, "Lord, I will follow You, but let me first go and bid them farewell who are at my house." But Jesus said to him, "No one, hav-*

ing put his hand to the plow, and looking back, is fit for the kingdom of God" (Luke 9:57–62)

And before you say yes to Jesus, listen to His words in Luke 14.

"For which of you, intending to build a tower, does not sit down first and count the cost, whether he has enough to finish it—lest, after he has laid the foundation, and is not able to finish, all who see it begin to mock him" (vv. 28, 29)

Having been in the real estate and development business during my career I have seen many structures partially completed and sitting for months or years, with some even being razed. Pretty well worthless and useless!

I'll conclude with one of the defining moments in my life. Some thirty years ago, my wife and I plus three other couples were meeting regularly as a group. Our assignment included reading and discussing a book; *Intercessor* by Rees Howells. He was a Welshman at a spiritually dark time in the history of Wales. The biography reveals a lifetime of progressive yielding to the Lord. God had big things in store for him and his nation. Toward the end of the book, the scene is revealed wherein the Spirit challenges Rees by asking him if he was willing to trust God for everything in his life. Rees contemplates this enormous decision and answers that he as a man could not answer absolutely. The Spirit gave him thirty days to ponder and respond. After the time passed, the Spirit engaged him again and asked the same question. Rees answered that he in all good conscience could not but the answer he did give impacted me significantly. He said: "I don't think I can say I am willing, but I am willing to be made willing." That was all the Spirit of God wished to hear, and now wishes to hear from us.

I am making the assumption you have said, "yes" to Jesus at this point or earlier in your life. So, to what is it He is calling you and me? *"I will make you fishers of men."* We could discuss this in detail here but I believe it is sufficient to say it is *"making disciples"* which we will fully address next.

QUESTIONS TO CONSIDER:

Do you believe He is addressing every Christian?

Have you ever thought about this command by Jesus as it relates to you?

If so, how has it impacted you and your daily walk?

If not, what will it take to have you address this seriously?

How can He use you in this area of your life?

What steps do you need to take be more effective in this area of your ministry?

Are you 'willing to be made willing?'

CHAPTER THREE
GO!

THIRD COMMAND:

*"Go therefore and make disciples of all the nations,
baptizing them in the name of the Father and of
the Son and of the Holy Spirit, teaching them to
observe all things I have commanded you..."*

(Matthew 28:19, 20a)

T HE COMMAND FROM THE LORD JESUS IS TO "GO and make disciples." "But, go where? And how am I to be going? I've got three kids, a wife, bills to pay and a shaky job at best." Another might say, "I'm a single parent and the stress to even get by is so consuming; how will I have time to fit in anything else?" Or, "I'm a college kid and I've got to make my grades or my dad will kill me." Then there is the corporate president who has more responsibility than two people can handle. "Maybe I could just make donations to mission groups who could do this." All remind me of myself years ago until God took hold of my heart and started showing me His plan, and the specific one He had for me. Maybe you find yourself in one of these categories, or something similar, like; "Isn't that the job of the pastors? They get paid to do that." And for many of us in the work world: "I know it is important and when I retire I'll begin to do that." Some of us even ponder full–time ministry as the answer. "If I were a missionary, discipleship would be really a vital part of my work."

But if one examines the Scriptures carefully, all these reasons/excuses lose their meaning. Nowhere does it say in theses verses or elsewhere that we have to "get our act together," go into "full-time ministry," wait till better times or even retirement. What it does say is "go make disciples." And clearly it has not excluded one person from this command who is a believer. See, Jesus called us, is equipping us, has us right where He wants us to complete the mission He's given us and He says: "Bloom where you're planted!"

The truest interpretation of the command to go is: "as you are going" or "as you are living." So many Christians look at this and take it to mean, "when God sends me, I will then consider going." And it usually is translated in our minds as some forsaken part of the world where I don't speak the language and have no clue as to their culture. Short or long–term mission trips are fabulous and necessary today. But that is only a part of the command. It is really saying—while I am in school, during my career, in spite of my circumstances I am to go make disciples. May I be bold and say here—we don't have an option to not "go and make disciples." He has made it abundantly imperative. Not to punish or burden us, but to fulfill us and receive joy along our life's journey. Listen to Jesus.

> *"These things I have spoken to you, that My joy may remain in you, and that your joy may be full"* (John 15:11)

Anyone into joy nowadays? The world certainly doesn't provide much, at least not lasting joy!

Consider this! The Lord of the universe has saved you, and He wants to bless you by including you in His plan for the world—to please His and our Father. Of course, all this has to be taken by faith. It is not something where one receives instant gratification. You'll receive a lot along the way, but the eternal rewards are countless. Just imagine, using some sanctified imagination, standing with Jesus one day in heaven discussing "eternal things" with the Father. He starts commending you for the hundreds or thousands of people who had been discipled directly or indirectly by you while on earth. Jesus is going on about your impact. You turn to Him in humility and disbelief as you only recall two or three people with whom you ever spent any amount of time for the purpose of discipleship. You are not wanting to question your Lord, and about that time He speaks. "Son, you never knew but each one of your disciples caught the vision completely and produced thousands of grandchildren, great grandchildren and beyond in the kingdom. You were so faithful to obey My command and look at the awesome results." You think, WOW!!! I never knew all that took place. But He responds; "I know, My son, but We did!"

How many of us can even imagine the "joy?" And for eternity at that! Well, it starts now, not then. What are we going to spend our available time doing? Watching sports, traveling the world, playing cards or golf, complaining about how life is not fair—you name it! Making disciples requires *discipline*. You have to dedicate yourself to it. *Prayer* is essential so the Spirit is free to direct those your way that need you, and only you. It may be a friend or peer, an employee, someone you just met and hit it off or a person who hears of your availability and pursues you. The Spirit is the one directing the divine appointments. Your responsibility is *availability* and *obedience*.

What is a *disciple*? Simply, it is a learner, but much more. My four years of Latin did teach me that *discipula* is student or pupil, one who is being taught that which is to be learned. Dr. John Tolson defines a disciple in three ways.

> ***Learner:*** True learning, Biblically speaking, only takes place when it changes the way you live.

Follower: Someone who 'sticks to' the person who is leading and teaching them.

Reproducer: Someone who duplicates themselves in others.

Dr. Ramesh Richard, Founder and President of RREACH, developed the Global Proclamation Academy in Dallas, TX. Each year 25 pastors from across the world are invited to attend a three-week intensive training program in conjunction with Dallas Theological Seminary where he is a professor. They are trained, challenged, ordained and sent back to their countries to pastor their people. But equally important is their call to reproduce (multiply) themselves in the lives of other men inside their country. True discipleship!

Discipleship then is the act or process of learning about the teachings of another, internalizing them and then acting upon them. Christian discipleship would necessarily focus on the teachings of Jesus Christ.

And a *disciple maker* is one who teaches and leads someone.

In my lifetime I don't think I have ever known anyone who impacted more lives through true discipleship than Allen Stickney. He and Alice served in Africa for years as well as in Dallas. I knew him through close friends of mine but I mostly knew him through the testimonies of men he had discipled in his lifetime. At his memorial service a few short years ago, evidence of his discipleship echoed from men throughout the celebration of his life. A vast majority of men in that large church were his spiritual descendants. One disciple, Jim Williams, Jr., shared a short but profound thought about Allen. 'He would look you in the eye and then touch your chest with his forefinger and ask, "How's it going in there?"' It was as if the hand of Jesus was opening your heart.' Testimony after testimony gave evidence of how Allen's time, and love, had been poured into them; and they in turn had passed it on through investment in many others. Can you even imagine the inexpressible joy that Allen sensed when he heard Jesus say—"WELL DONE, Allen!"

"Better caught than taught" is an okay expression but making disciples really involves both. Look closely at Jesus and His earthly life. He is our true example. Twelve men were chosen (more came along) and He poured His life and teachings into them. Want to guess the number of offspring accredited to these men? Try billions and counting! But we all know that up and until Pentecost, these guys were wimping out at the "caught and taught" game. But when the Holy Spirit was ushered into their lives, it was a whole new ballgame. Jesus said, *"Nevertheless I tell you the truth. It is to your advantage that I go away; for if I do not go away, the Helper will not come to you; but if I depart, I will send Him to you....However, when He, the Spirit of truth, has come, He will guide you into all truth; for He will not speak on His own authority, but whatever He hears He will speak; and He will tell you things to come. He will glorify Me, for He will take of what is Mine and declare it to you"* (John 16:7, 13, 14).

Jesus also said, *"Most assuredly I say to you, he who believes in Me, the works I do he will do also; and greater works than these he will do, because I go to My Father. And whatever you ask in My name, that will I do, that the Father may be glorified in the Son"* (John 14:12, 13). And the reason Jesus could say that you and I would do greater things than He did is because after His ascension He would be mobilizing our work in the power and presence of His Holy Spirit.

> *"These things I have spoken to you while being present with you. But the Helper, the Holy Spirit, whom the Father will send in My name, He will teach you all things, and bring to your remembrance all things that I said to you"* (John 14:25, 26)

He knew He had to go away so the Spirit could be poured out on the ones called to be a part of His kingdom. By doing so, the prophecy in Joel 2:28, 29 would be fulfilled.

"And it shall come to pass afterward that I will pour out My Spirit on all flesh; your sons and daughters shall prophesy, your old men shall dream dreams, your young men shall see visions. And also on My menservants and on My maidservants I will pour out My Spirit in those days."

The "Church" was born/given life on the first Pentecost—fifty days after Easter Sunday (Resurrection). It is recorded in Acts 2:1–4. That day, the command to "make disciples" began officially and with power, and continues today.

How and where come to mind? Let's address the *how* first. Since Jesus was the true disciple–maker we might look at His methods. He...

- Called men to Himself—He was observant for followers
- Called them to repentance—they were aware of the need
- Spent time with them—He loved them
- Taught them truth—He was diligent for the word
- Prayed with and for them—He demonstrated its value
- Demanded obedience—they saw its necessity

- Showed the need to serve—they saw mercy/grace in Him
- Sent them out—He got them out of their comfort zone

Jesus was fully God and yet during His three plus discipleship years, He was dependent on God's Spirit. This was evidenced by the Spirit descending on Him at His baptism by John (Mark 1:10). For you and me to be a disciple–maker, we have to be filled by the same Holy Spirit. Because it is actually He who is doing the work through us.

Now to the *where* question.

"You shall be witnesses to Me in Jerusalem, in all Judea and Samaria, and to the end of the earth" (Acts 1:8b)

I find it interesting that only seven chapters later, in Acts 8:1, there was a great persecution on the church in Jerusalem and they were scattered throughout the regions of Judea and Samaria. And it tells us in verse 4 that; *"those who were scattered went everywhere preaching the word."* No doubt God knew something the disciples didn't at Pentecost. The persecution was God's instrument to drive them out of their "comfort zone" to the ends of the earth. But He had equipped them through Jesus and now through the power and presence of the Spirit. They said "yes;" He said "go!" And go they did.

So, what does that tell us here in America? You say, "But I don't live in the Middle East. What do those places have to do with me?" Let's see. *Jerusalem* may represent your home and close community. *Judea* may be the surrounding region of your part of the world, and *Samaria* just might be people of a different color and culture. The first experience of the "end of the earth" for me was in 2008 in parts of India. We went by car as far as we could and then by foot to villages where the name of Jesus had never been heard. I remember reflecting—this is the end of the earth! People trusted Christ and were made a part of a small church for the local evangelists and pastors to disciple.

Very early one morning in 1986 God shared a vision with me. Over a three-hour period He repeatedly said—"I want to build a spiritual house in the real estate community of Dallas." 1 Peter 2:5 is the foundational verse for what became and now exists as Dallas Real Estate Ministries (DREM).

> *"You also, as living stones, are being built up a spiritual house, a holy priesthood, to offer up spiritual sacrifices acceptable to God through Jesus Christ."*

One of the key elements inside DREM is Mission Marketplace. Craig Bess, Director of CrossTrainers, is leading these men who have not left their business world but are actively making disciples. The eventual goal is to disciple 5,000 men. Men discipling men right where they live and work!

As a parent, especially fathers, with children, you have been given disciples directly from God's hand to train and equip in the Lord. And grandparents, aunts and uncles; you have a continuing role here. Men, there is your wife. Teachers, students, businessmen and women, service agencies, factory workers; all of you have a "circle of influence" in which He has placed you. There are neighbors, people at your worship center, kids you coach, small groups you lead and ministries in which you serve. NO EXCUSES!!! And no lack of opportunities. As you go! As you live your life! Make disciples. It may even start with and include evangelism. A critical point here; God saves; we disciple! But we all should be equipped to share the gospel with a non–believer. I learned this through the Evangelism Explosion program and later the ministry of Evantell. It will take you no more than four concentrated hours to learn these evangelism techniques. Barna reports that only 55% of all evangelical Christians in

America have ever shared the gospel with another person. [10]

I recall hearing the late Dr. James Kennedy, pastor of Coral Ridge Presbyterian Church and founder of Evangelism Explosion say that only 5% of Christians in America have ever led someone to a saving knowledge of Christ. I find this statistic to be shameful and yet challenging.

The apostle Paul proclaims; *"For I am not ashamed of the gospel of Christ, for it is the power of God to salvation for everyone who believes, for the Jew first and also for the Greek"* (Romans 1:16). Later in I Corinthians 15 he clearly explains the gospel in a few early verses 1–4. To sum up his words: *Christ died for our sins and rose from the dead.* Many of us believe it is adequate to just live a "good life" never dishonoring Christ. And that is partly okay but far from the role of a slave to Christ. You and I have been purchased by the shed blood of our Savior Jesus; we no longer belong to ourselves. We are "slaves" in every sense of the word. We can choose to disobey and be miserable or we can obey and receive His boundless joy. It's a choice you and I have to make. We had absolutely nothing to do with being "reborn," but we do as it relates to our obedience and sanctification (becoming more like Jesus,

---

[10] Website: http://www.barna.org/barna-update/article/5-barna-update/186-survey-shows-how-christians-share-their-faith. Accessed August 20, 2014.

see Romans 8:29). He was having an intimate time with His disciples before His departure back to the Father as recorded in the 13th–15th chapter of John. He sums it up in John 14; *"He who has my commandments and keeps them, it is he who loves me. And he who loves Me will be loved by My Father, and I will love him and manifest Myself to him"* (v. 21). The statement says to me that love reflects obedience; and obedience reflects love, somewhat indicating they are synonymous. James said it another way.

> *"But do you want to know, O foolish man, that faith without works is dead"* (James 2:20)

By obeying God and His commands we are showing our love toward Him just the same as works give credibility to our faith.

In John 15 we see the parable of the vine and the branches. There are four persons addressed. First, those who are producing no fruit; second, some fruit; then the second ones are pruned and produce more fruit; and finally the ones who are abiding produce much fruit. No fruit, some fruit, more fruit, much fruit! Where are you?

Being "fishers of men" and "making disciples" should become as routine as inhaling and exhaling. These are unconscious natural actions providing and sustaining our physical lives. The life of the body of Christ must have the same life–producing action, for without disciple making, it will die a natural death. We are responsible for our generation and the next. What we do in the "dash" period between our birth and death will determine the health of the Body. Jesus will accomplish His Father's will; He has promised that. The question is: "Will you and I be a part of it?" Or will we choose to let "clerical George" do it? Don't wait on the next guy! Step up, sell out and say *YES!* to Jesus.

Dr. John Tolson in his book, *The Four Priorities*, offers four excellent and practical expectations in a discipleship relationship. (p. 266)

A. *Intentional Participants.* Each disciple should have a willingness to commit on the front end to disciple two people per year. As a disciple-maker, your time is valuable. If you invest your time into another person, that person should be willing to make the same commitment to others (and request the same commitment from those they disciple!)

B. *Meet weekly.* Frequency in meeting helps with accountability and follow-through.

C. *Come prepared.* The discipleship relationship is a mutually transforming relationship. The disciple-maker and the disciple should arrive having read the chapter and be ready to actively discuss the insights gained through the study and application of the material.

D. *Consistent application.* Both the disciple and disciple-maker should leave the meeting time committed to applying the lessons learned in each chapter.

Paul challenged his young and faithful disciple, Timothy.

"And the things that you have heard from me among many witnesses, commit these to faithful men who will be able to teach others also" (2 Timothy 2:2)

It's our road map!

Alone, you and I can't, but with Him, all things are possible. Which brings us to the last segment of this book; "the promise backed by authority!"

QUESTIONS TO CONSIDER:

Have you ever been discipled by anyone?

Have you ever discipled anyone?

Are you willing to be made willing?

Will you pray right now that God would lead you to someone to disciple you and someone for you to disciple?

CHAPTER FOUR
THE PROMISE!

And Jesus came and spoke to them, saying,
"All authority has been given to Me in heaven
and on earth...and lo, I am with you always,
even to the end of the age"
(Matthew 28:18, 20b)

J ESUS HAD EARLIER TOLD THEM TO GO TO GALILEE AS he would meet them there. The eleven disciples along with others were present. Matthew records that, *"When they saw Him, they worshiped Him; but some doubted"* (v. 28:17). This will always be the case. The challenge is: Will you and I live as a "believer" or a "doubter?" He spoke to that doubt in the verses recorded above. We know it as the Great Commission. Maybe we should do as the father of the demon–possessed son when addressing Jesus about healing his son and the matter of his faith.

"Lord, I believe; help my unbelief!" (Mark 9.24b)

Jesus' "promise with authority" assures success; even when we fail, and we will at times fail. 'Failing does not mean that you are a failure.' What did He really say?

He has all authority—
Both in heaven and on earth,
He is with us—
Always, and
Even to the end of the age.

Our Lord said He would make us fishers of men. The burden is on Him, not us. We are only to be obedient vessels through which He accomplishes His work. Do you see the image of the body of Christ, you and me, the Church? And He is working out His plan through all of us. And He said for us to make disciples of all nations but with the complete confidence and assurance He would be there with us. *The only way we can fail is not to obey.* In Philippians 2 we see the eternal plan revealed in living color.

"Let this mind be in you which was also in Christ Jesus, who, being in the form of God, did not consider it robbery to be equal with God, but made Himself of no reputation, taking the form of a bondservant, and coming in the likeness of men. And being found in ap-

pearance as a man, He humbled Himself and became obedient to the point of death, even the death of the cross. Therefore God also has highly exalted Him and given Him the name which is above every name, that at the name of Jesus every knee should bow, of those in heaven, and of those on earth, and of those under the earth, and that every tongue should confess that Jesus Christ is Lord, to the glory of God the Father" (Philippians 2:5–11)

No further explanation is needed. Jesus is our model; but He is more importantly our Lord. It is His domain, not ours. We are His slaves, available and looking for that next opportunity to serve Him and please Him, to the glory of the Father. The message in verses 12 and 13 is for you and me.

"Therefore, my beloved, as you have always obeyed, not as in my presence only, but now much more in my absence, work out your own salvation with fear and trembling; for it is God who works in you both to will and to do for His good pleasure."

We are the bearers of His light in a dark and dying world. He has "recruited" us, rather saved us for His pleasure. Paul really paints a clear picture of what all of us should be about daily. It is found in Colossians 1:28, 29:

> *"Him we preach, warning every man and teaching every man in all wisdom, that we may present every man perfect in Christ Jesus. To this end I also labor, striving according to His working which works in me mightily."*

And do you see how Paul accomplishes the mission of "warning and teaching" (disciple–making)? He <u>labors</u>, <u>even striving</u>, but it is done *<u>"according to His working which works in me mightily."</u>* Yes, we play our part, even diligently; but it is performed "according to His working." This should give us great comfort and confidence.

Let's sum up what we have been discussing so as to leave a clear picture for us to meditate on before closing out our adventure into the mind of God. The Great Commission is best described in this way.

1) *The announcement:* The Messiah rules! God wins!
2) *The commission:* Make disciples! Those who love and follow Jesus.
3) *The means:* Baptize and teach! Passionate embrace of the heart.

4) *The promise:* He is present! Emmanuel, God with us.

Responsibility and desire need to be examined. We know that our responsibility to Christ will be derailed by our own personal desires unless we identify them and bring them under the lordship of Christ.

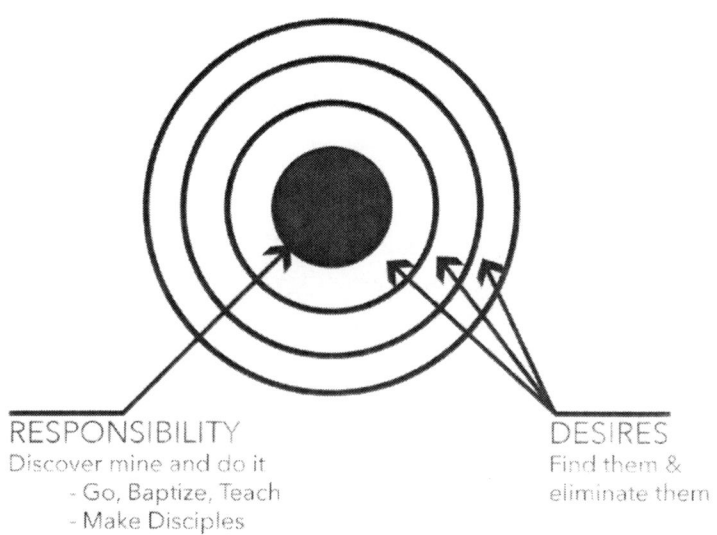

RESPONSIBILITY
Discover mine and do it
- Go, Baptize, Teach
- Make Disciples

DESIRES
Find them &
eliminate them

Jesus saw people through a compassionate heart. He is calling us to do the same. I confess that too many times I see people from a judgmental viewpoint and not as "souls" in need of a Savior or Lord. There is an expression I first heard from my former pastor, Dr. Joseph "Skip" Ryan: *"What goes deepest to the heart goes widest to the world."* God's heart is for the lost. Do I "see" as Jesus sees; do you? I conclude with a challenge. But first, meditate on what Jesus says in Matthew 9:36–38. It says it all!

But when He saw the multitudes, He was moved with compassion for them, because they were weary and scattered, like sheep having no shepherd. Then He said to His disciples, "The harvest truly is plentiful, but the laborers are few. Therefore pray the Lord of the harvest to send out laborers into His harvest."

QUESTIONS TO CONSIDER:

Are you available to the Lord to fulfill His Commission?

Do you believe He can use you?

If so, how is He going to use you?

Why is His promise so necessary to your success?

Christ's work moves from one generation to another. Each has to be faithful in their obedience to Him. His Second Coming at the "end of the age" which we should long for and be prepared to receive will not happen until every nation, tongue and tribe have heard the name of Jesus and the gospel. Will we be that generation to usher Him back? I say we can and should be. As my friend John Maisel, Founder of East–West Ministries, often says; "ninety-five percent is just showing up." John, I agree! It is primarily His work; He just chose us to do it through. So, "as we are going," are we making room for Him along the way and are we yielding our lives and schedules to His Spirit for the sake of the Kingdom? Another friend and Founder of Evantell, Larry Moyer, the founder of Evantell, Inc. in Dallas reminds us that *"We don't bring people to Christ, we bring Christ to people."* And I would add, *as we are going!*

The gift of the Holy Spirit to us is the fulfillment of His last words on earth before His ascension; ***"and lo, I am with you always, even to the end of the age"*** (Matthew 28:20b). I second Matthew's last thought—Amen! Which means "I agree." No less than five times Jesus tells the disciples and the crowds that He has come ***"to seek and save that which was lost"*** (Luke 19:10). That's us! That's family, friends, associates, and passengers next to us, neighbors, and peers; yes, even enemies. Maybe even people in the pews and our Sunday school class. The Spirit is our "agent for obedience." We are fearful, He is not; we are ashamed, He is not; we are timid; believe me, He is not! Whatever is weak in us that keeps us from engaging in Kingdom work, that is the place where He can exhibit His strength. We must confess these to Him and ask for His power and presence. After all, it is His work that counts for eternity anyway—we are just the earthly vessel, planting and watering. What can man do to us that can harm us? Nothing!

There is a line in the movie, *Facing the Giants that* my family reminded me of recently. The coach poses the question to this young student/athlete—"What is impossible with God?" The youngster answered without wavering—"Nothing coach!" And he is right. The barriers and hurdles we face in the areas of our obedience are nothing to the Spirit. The only barrier to Him, unfortunately, is our lack of faith. The Spirit through the writer of Hebrews sets it out very clearly to us.

> *"But without faith it is impossible to please Him (God)"* (v. 11:6a)

We all want to please our Heavenly Father and His Son. But many of us "err on the side of caution." He doesn't! We need to live dangerously, not recklessly, but without fear; boldly, for Jesus. There is an expression I hear and use a lot—"I had rather ask forgiveness than permission."

If I take Jesus' last words seriously and at face value, then there is nothing to fear but fear itself. All other enemies are defeated, even death. This is a promotion to the believer. How do I turn fear into faith? A story that might make the point. A few seasons back my eldest grandson and his six-man football team were traveling to play their fiercest competitor. This was the last game of a good season but the opponent had soundly defeated them the past several years. It was their 'bowl game' so to speak. There was no evidence that Luke's team would fare any differently this night. You could see the fear in their eyes. How would they respond? The coach and the leaders somehow turned their fear into faith! They went out and played with a vengeance, executing well. By the half there was no doubt who was going to win. It was a blowout! *Fear was defeated and faith was rewarded!* I might add that three years later, in 2012, this same group of young men won the school's first state championship and believe they can repeat in 2013. They did! Back to back!

Paul said; *"for to me, to live is Christ, but to die is gain"* (Philippians 1:21). He goes on to say: *"But if I live on in the flesh, this will mean fruit from my labor..."* (v. 22a). That is what we each should desire— fruit from our labor. I submit Christ gave us the formula for this in <u>His three crucial commands accented by His promise.</u>

1) **Repent**
2) **Follow Me**
3) **Go, making disciples**
4) **I am with you always**

It is not a one–time decision; it is a lifetime commitment!! And it is worked out daily in our lives. There is a blessed and necessary rhythm to life in the Kingdom. We have everything we need for success.

1) **Word**
2) **Prayer**
3) **Fellowship**
4) **Holy Spirit**

This combination cannot fail. But you know what these ingredients need to work? HEAT! You can put raw ingredients for a cake in bowl; you can stir and beat it till you're exhausted and it doesn't make a cake. Only until they are placed in a pan, put in the oven and exposed to the heat will the desired outcome be produced. Same with us—we may have all the ingredients we need to produce a victorious life in Christ, but until we enter the fray in people's lives for Him, armed with His weapons, we will be a miserable failure. Do you wish to "stay in the bowl" and eventually sour; or, or do you want to "get into the oven" where the action will produce a fisher of men; where you are making disciples. A good cake baker pulls it out of the oven and he/she and others admire the end result. He has put in you the correct ingredients in the right sized bowl. He has mixed you well with others in the world. He has put the oven on the right heat level for you, and like any good chef, He has watched over you to the end for the best possible results. And when you are finished—you will hear Him say **"WELL DONE!!!"** Do you think it is worth all you can give to hear those words? One last question—are you living with the end result in sight? It is said that there are only two days in a believer's life—Today and That Day. Are we living Today with That Day in mind? If so, and I pray that you are—then be about His crucial commands daily!

REPENT—FOLLOW ME—GO!

QUESTIONS TO CONSIDER:

Have your ideas of "go" in this command been in line with the thoughts in this chapter?

Do you agree or disagree and why for either?

Do you believe "making disciples" applies to all Christians?

Does it apply to you?

Is this Great Commission a priority in your life?

What would it take to make it a top priority?

What is your view of the work of the Holy Spirit in the church's life? — in your life?

What difference does it make to have Jesus promise He will be with you to the end of the age?

And in your role as a disciple–maker?

AFTERWORD

H OPEFULLY, YOU WERE CHALLENGED READING *Three Crucial Commands of Christ with a Promise* and were blessed by the material. But, we should never lose sight of the overwhelming evidence that the Source/Author of our mission in life, including the family, is God, the Creator. His only Son, Jesus the Christ, was there in the beginning with the Father and the Holy Spirit. Old and New Testament Scriptures speak clearly about the issue. In John 1:3 the apostle tells us *"All things were made through Him (Son), and without Him nothing was made that was made."* He goes on to say in vs. 4 that *"In Him was life; and the life was the light of men."*

And in Hebrews 1, parts of vv. 1 and 2 tell us *"God...has in these last days spoken to us by His Son, whom He has appointed heir of all things, through whom also He made the worlds."* Jesus said of Himself in John 14.6; *"...I am the way, the truth and the life. No one comes to the Father, except through Me."*

All of His creation speaks of His eternal qualities and majesty. We have but to gaze at the miracles of life each day to see it. Maybe for the first time, or in a deeper sense, you drew nearer to God through the moments you read and pondered on His Word. Possibly, He spoke specifically to you, and there is now a desire for you to know Him more intimately. He said through His servant James in 4.8a: *"Draw near to God, and He will draw near to you."* How do I do that?

The gospel message summarized from 1 Corinthians 15:1–8 is: *Christ died for our sins and rose from the dead.* [11]

> *"for all have sinned and fall short of the glory of God."* (Romans 3:23)

> *"For the wages of sin is death, but the free gift of God is eternal life in Jesus Christ our Lord."* (Romans 6:23)

> *"But God demonstrates His own love toward us, in that while we were yet sinners, Christ died for us."* (Romans 5:8)

> *"For by grace you have been saved through faith; and that not of yourselves, it is the gift of God; not as a result of works, that no one should boast."* (Ephesians 2:8, 9)

---

[11] Summary of the gospel message by R. Larry Moyer, founder of Evantell, Inc., Dallas, Texas.

And in John 5:24 we see a truth that can be embraced through faith (trust) in Jesus who tells you and me…*"Most assuredly, I say to you, he who hears My word, and believes in Him who sent Me, <u>has</u> everlasting life, and shall not come into judgment, but <u>has passed</u> out of death into <u>life</u>."* He spoke clearly again in John 11:25 when He said, *"I am the resurrection, and the life. He who believes in Me, though he may die, he shall live."*

If you have never, and it is the desire of your heart to trust Jesus Christ for your salvation and to partake in His eternal life, then the following prayer would be a suggested way for you to take that step today. Read over the prayer and if it reflects your wishes, then pray it right now. Know that it is not the prayer that saves, but placing your trust in Christ alone for your salvation.

> *"Dear God, I know I'm a sinner. I know my sin deserves to be punished. I believe Christ died for me and rose from the grave. I trust Jesus Christ alone as my Savior. Thank you for the forgiveness and everlasting life I now have. In Jesus' name, amen."*

Welcome to the Kingdom of God! Did you hear the angels rejoicing? Well, they are!

Eternal life is based on fact, not feeling. *Now…*

1) Tell God what is on your mind through prayer—Philippians 4:6, 7.
2) Read the Bible daily—2 Timothy 3:16, 17—Start with the Book of John.
3) Worship with God's people in a local Christ-centered church—Hebrews 10:24, 25.
4) Learn to share the gospel and tell others about Jesus Christ—Matthew 4:19.
5) Go and make disciples—Matthew 28:18-20

It has been said that in order to be a vital part of fulfilling God's Great Commission as stated in Matthew 28:18–20, one has to first be about addressing His Great Commandment as spoken by Christ (quoting from Leviticus and Deuteronomy) in Matthew 22:37–40.

> *"…You shall love the LORD your God with all your heart, with all your soul, and with all your mind. This is the first and great commandment. And the second is like it: 'You shall love your neighbor as yourself.' On these two commandments hang all the Law and the Prophets."*

First, we must humbly receive salvation through Christ alone (be justified by) and then proceed on the road of sanctification through obedience to His word by the indwelling presence of the Holy Spirit. We must decrease as He increases.

The best place to start your discipleship mission is with your own family. You might even find they have been praying for you for some time. Rejoice together!

CPSIA information can be obtained at www.ICGtesting.com
Printed in the USA
LVOW11s1216201114

414351LV00001BA/1/P